Invest Ultimate Guide From Novice To Expert

Invest Intelligently To Six Figures

JONATHAN S. WALKER

DEDICATION

I dedicate this book to my two beautiful children and my loving wife who have been nothing short of being my light and joy throughout the years.

Furthermore, the transmission, duplication or reproduction of any of the following work including specific information will be considered an illegal act irrespective of if it is done electronically or in print. This extends to creating a secondary or tertiary copy of the work or a recorded copy and is only allowed with express written consent from the Publisher. All additional right reserved.

The information in the following pages is broadly considered to be a truthful and accurate account of facts and as such any inattention, use or misuse of the information in question by the reader will render any resulting actions solely under their purview. There are no scenarios in which the publisher or the original author of this work can be in any fashion deemed liable for any hardship or damages that may befall them after undertaking information described herein.

Additionally, the information in the following pages is intended only for informational purposes and should thus be thought of as universal. As befitting its nature, it is presented without assurance regarding its prolonged validity or interim quality. Trademarks that are mentioned are done without written consent and can in no way be considered an endorsement from the trademark holder.

VIP Subscriber List

Dear Reader, If you would like to receive latest tips and tricks on internet marketing, exclusive strategies, upcoming books & promotions, and more, do subscribe to my mailing list in the link below! I will be giving away a free book that you can download right away as well after you subscribe to show my appreciation!

Here's the link: http://bit.do/jonathanswalker

CONTENTS

Introduction

Congratulations on purchasing your personal copy of *Investor's Ultimate Guide From Novice to Expert: Invest Intelligently to Six Figures.* Thank you for doing so.

The following chapters will discuss some of the many things that you are able to do in order to grow your investment and to start making six figures in no time. The guidebook will start with some information on penny stocks, such as what penny stocks are, some of the best strategies to do well in penny stocks and how to pick the stocks that will help you to make the best decision to make money even as a beginner.

Next, we will move on to learning about some of the other investment opportunities that you can choose from t make a lot of money. We will talk about some of the basics of picking out an investment, the different types that you can pick such as bonds, the stock market, and real estate, and then some of the strategies that you can use no matter what investment you choose to go with.

When it is time to make your money grow and you want to replace your regular income, investing is the option for you. Take a look through this guidebook and learn some of the basics that you need to know about penny stocks, as well as some of the other investment types so that you can start making money today!

There are plenty of books on this subject on the market, thanks again for choosing this one! Every effort was made to ensure it is full of as much useful information as possible. Please enjoy!

Part 1: Penny Stocks

Chapter 1: What are Penny Stocks?

Penny stocks are relatively simple, but there are a few tricks that you need to learn in order to make them work for your needs. They represent stocks that are going to have a low price, usually a price that is under a dollar, as well as a smaller market cap that is under $500 million. For the most part, when an investor is working with penny stocks, they are going to be traded off of the traditional exchanges, so you will not find them on the New York Stock Exchange or on the NASDAQ.

So why would you want to choose to work with penny stocks rather than another investment type? There are several reasons to use penny stocks, but they are often used in order to help a company procure the right capital so that the company can grow and become more powerful. Through this market, the company is able to build up the money that is needed so they can grow their business and when you pick the right company, they can make a strong investment for a low cost.

Penny stocks are going to be traded in order to benefit some of the smaller public companies. But if this company does well, and you purchased the stock over the counter before it entered the regular stock exchanges, you could get a great return on investment. Even if the company never makes it over to the regular stock exchange, many of these can still increase their profits and you can earn back on your investment.

Almost all of the penny stocks are going to be sold on over the counter exchanges. This is going to work because many of the larger exchanges are going to have stringent policies before a company can join them and trade. Most of the companies that are in penny stocks will come nowhere near reaching these stringent requirements, plus it costs a lot of money to trade on these exchanges, so it isn't possible for some smaller companies to make it work. Instead of trying to meet some of these requirements or come up with large amounts of money that they don't have, the companies are going to work with the penny stocks to get the funding they need. As the investor, you are able to capitalize on this and get some great stocks, often from some growing companies, for a low price.

As the investor, you need to remember that there will be some risk that comes with going with penny stocks. If you take the time to educate yourself and learn how to avoid some of the major mistakes that come with this investment, you are more likely to make a good income in the process, but keep in mind there are some risks and they are sometimes seen as speculative in nature, rather than as an investment.

Benefits of going with penny stocks

First, let's take some time to look at the benefits of going with penny stocks. Penny stocks could be your next big break. They are a lot of fun to work with because there are a lot of companies who are out there and are looking to use penny stocks as a way to raise capital to grow and become big. If you pick out the right company, you could be one of the first people in on it, and that stock that you got for under a dollar will end up being worth a lot of money down the road if the company does grow.

That is one of the main benefits that come with investing is that there is the potential of making a huge return on investment. You need to make sure that you purchase a stock that is at a low price, which is easy to do in penny stocks, and make sure that it has a good business plan and will survive the market, just like you would with any other investment, and you will see results. Not all companies that are in penny stocks will make it to the big leagues, but many of them can still grow and you can make money from this process.

Many investors like to go with penny stocks because they are exciting and a lot of fun to work with. It is fun and can feel great, to start out with a little bit of money and then move up and see it grow. You may not make a ton of money at first, but penny stocks can help you to start with a small investment and get it to grow. If you want to start out your portfolio and you don't have a ton of money for it, penny stocks can be a great place to start.

The negatives of penny stocks

One of the first negatives that you should be aware of when you are working in penny stocks is that many of the companies on the market are not that good. There are some companies who are really good and just need to make a few tweaks or make a bit more profit before they are able to join the regular stock markets. But many of the companies that you will find in penny stocks didn't get onto the major stock exchanges because they were just bad. You need to learn how to tell the difference between the two if you would like to make an income here.

In addition, the penny stock market is not as reliable as the major stock markets. They are unreliable and they often don't have regulations in place to determine which companies or transactions that go on with them. This doesn't mean that all of the companies are bad on the penny stock market, but since there aren't really a lot of regulations that are in place, many bad companies can sneak through, make up numbers, or hide information and it is really risky picking out the company you want to work with. You will need to be diligent and really do your research to make sure that you are picking out good companies that will earn you money over time.

Penny stocks are really interesting investments to make. They usually have stocks that come in under a dollar each, so they are a good choice for those who have limited money to invest with in the beginning. While you do need to be on guard against some of the bad companies that are able to get onto the penny stock exchange, there are still many great ones that are available that you can pick from and that will help you to make a good return on your investment!

Chapter 2: Picking the Right Trading Strategies

When it comes to working in penny stocks, or any other investment for that matter, one of the most important things that you will need to do is figure out the strategy that you want to use. The strategy is so important because it is going to determine which stocks you will purchase when you will purchase them and sell them, and what research you will do to get the results. There are many great strategies that are available and none of them are necessarily any better or worse than the others, but you will find that picking a strategy and sticking with it, rather than bouncing back and forth between a few, can make all the difference. Some of the best trading strategies that you can use when you want to trade in penny stocks include:

Scalping

This is often a popular strategy to go with because it is pretty simple to use and many beginners like this simplicity. With the idea of scalp trading, you are going to take advantage of some of the inefficiencies that are going on in the market with respect to the spread. The gap between the bid price and the asking price, which is known as the spread, can end up widening or narrowing rapidly throughout time, and even through the day and they are going to create some great selling and buying opportunities that will result in some quick profits.

To scalp, you will need to be good at watching the market and understanding the perfect time to purchase and sale. You can even look at a few markets and see if you are able to find the stocks of a company a little lower than the price of them on the other. You would then purchase the stock at the lower price before moving it over to the other market and selling it for the higher price that is demanded there. You can end up selling the stocks pretty quickly this way and while the profit may only be a little bit on each one, if you purchase quite a few stocks and do this many times, you can make a good profit.

Range trading

When things are going along as normal and all of the other things in the market are even, stocks are often going to trade inside of a set trading range each day. When you use range trading to help you to purchase and sell your penny stocks, you will try to purchase the stock when it is at the bottom of the range, and then when it gets to the top, you will want to sell it. To do this type of trading, you will want to make sure that the stocks have a consistent trading range each day so that you can make some good estimates.

So with this one, you are going to take a look at some of the history of the company, if it is available, and find out what places seem to be the high points of the stock and which ones seem to be the low points. There can be some variations of this each day, but mostly you will notice that the trend stays about the same. You will then take this information to help you make the right purchases on all of your stocks. You will be able to make a purchase of the stock when the market is at the low end of the range and then you can sell the stock when it goes back up before it goes down and you lose out again. This one will require you to spend some time looking through many graphs and charts to get the information, but it can be pretty straightforward and can make you a good profit.

Momentum trading

This is the trading option that you will go with if you are looking to go with some of the trends that are in the market to make a good profit. In basic terms, you are going to use momentum trading or trend trading to purchase a stock when it is trending up, but then you will sell the stock as soon as the trend starts to go back down. This one can be a little less risky compared to some of the others, but you have to constantly be watching the trends and the market to make sure that you get out before all of your investment is gone.

Real-time new trading.

Another option that you are able to go with when

you are working on penny stocks is known as real time news trading. This is the one where you are going to have to spend some time reading or watching the news and looking for some clues as to how a market or a particular company is going to do. When you find that some good news is released, you will make the purchase, and then after that little punch up, you will sell the stock. It can also work to protect your investment because if you notice that some bad news is about to happen, you can sell the stocks without losing all the money, and then purchase them again when things settle down.

If you want to use this kind of trading strategy, you will want to make sure that you download a real-time news feed so that you are always getting information in. You also need to be able to understand what each piece of news can mean to the penny stocks that you are working with. You don't want to misunderstand what is going on and end up with selling a stock that was going up or losing out on a stock because you held onto it for too long.

When it comes to picking out the strategy that you want to use for your penny stocks, you will find that there is really no wrong answer. Each person is going to pick out a different strategy to help them out, and what works for one person is not going to work for you. Make sure to check out some of these strategies and then pick the one that works the best for you!

Chapter 3: Getting Started with Your First Trade

When you are ready to get started with your first trade in penny stocks, you will need to take a couple of steps. First, it is important to figure out the broker that you would like to work with. there are many different brokers available out there and many of them have great reputations that can help you to get done with your trading. You should compare a few of them right from the beginning, looking at the features that they offer, as well as some of the fees and costs that they will hand down to you. These will all affect how easy it is to do trades with your broker and how much you will actually make.

Once you have chosen the broker you want to work with, it is time to pick the strategy that you want to work with as well. There are many different strategies, and we discussed a few of them in the chapter above. These can all be successful based on what you would like to get out of the trading. The most important option here is to learn about the different trading strategies for penny stocks and then stick with it.

Many of the investors who end up failing are the ones who just can't seem to stick with the trading strategy that they originally picked. These are the people who will bounce back and forth between a few different options, but they never get familiar or comfortable with just one of them. You can pick any of the strategies that you would like, but you need to make sure that you are sticking with it if you want to see results.

Next on the list is to choose the stocks that you would like to invest in. This is the part that is going to take some time and you will probably need to use your chosen strategy to help you make the right decisions. When you are picking a stock to invest in, especially when it comes to the penny stock market, you want to make sure that you are being really careful. This is a fantastic market to get into, but if you are not paying attention and doing your research, you will find that your money will be all gone. Many good companies get onto the penny stock market, but so do many bad ones so you have to be diligent if you want to see success.

There are a number of things that you can do to make sure you pick out the right stocks when working in the penny stock market. First, make sure to check out the numbers on your own. Most companies want to gain your trust and will put up their sales information and other relevant things to help you make a good decision to go with them. But since this is not always required of stocks on the penny stock market, there are some that may not provide this information at all and some that will hide factors or fudge the numbers a bit. Doing your own research, and being critical to see if that research is correct, can be a great way to ensure that you are picking out good stocks that will help you earn money.

Always be critical when it comes to picking out a stock on this market. There are too many new investors who are excited to get into the trading business and who want to be able to pick out a company that will make it big. But if you jump in too quickly and don't pay attention to what you are doing while trading, you are going to end up in trouble, and probably losing a lot of money. Make smart decisions, pick out stocks that you think will do well, and always go through and do your own research, and you are sure to see the results.

And finally, after you have chosen your strategy and the stocks that you want to invest in, you have to decide how much you want to invest. Since the penny stock market is often inexpensive, with many of the options coming in at under a dollar, it is pretty affordable for you to make some purchase and get started. But even so, you will want to set the maximum that you want to spend on the stocks, as well as how much you are willing to lose before you get out of the market. Having this plan in place ahead of time can help you to make informed decisions, rather than ones attached to your emotions, and you will see much less risk in the process.

Along the way, if you happen to have any questions about how things are working or what you should do, turning to your broker can be a great idea. They have a lot of experience working in the various investments so they should be able to answer any of the questions or the concerns that come up and they can lead you in the right direction to making a good return on your investment.

Part 2: Investors Ultimate Guide from Novice to Expert

Chapter 4: The Basics of Investing

Many people are interested in investing, but they are not sure what steps to take to get started. Many times the information that is available can be confusing and once they enter the market, it is just too much to handle. Luckily, investing doesn't have to be hard, you just need to understand how to get started. Let's take a look at some of the basics that come with investing so that you can get started.

What is investing?

first, investing is going to refer to business activities where an investor will spend money in order to gain a profit. The investment is supposed to help the investor to make money and increase the value of their money through some business activities. There are many different ways that you can do this. You can choose to start your own business and invest funds into that, you can invest in the stock market, you can choose real estate investing, and so much more. But whatever type of investment that you choose, there needs to be at least some chance of making the money back and even making a profit, otherwise, it is too risky to work with.

All of the methods above are great ways to help invest your money, you simply need to pick the one that works the best for you. You should also spend some time learning how to reduce the risk of your investment. For example, if you wanted to start a business, you would learn about the market, make a good product, and find ways to sell the product so that you can make a good profit without losing out on all of your money. If you just go into an investment without some planning, you are basically gambling rather than investing.

Before you decide to get into an investment, it is a good idea have a little bit of savings ready to go. If you make smart decisions on your investment, you shouldn't have too many issues with losing all of your money, but some investments, such as real estate, can be labor and time intensive and having some savings in hand ahead of time can reduce the risk and help reduce the stress. Then when you start to invest, make sure that a few your profits go back into your savings to help out as well.

In addition, this savings can be a great way to get started on your investment. Most of us don't have a ton of extra money lying around that we can use for this kind of investment. But if we take a few months and put a little bit back for savings, it is easier to reach our goals. Then we are able to start investing without having to cut into our income or the money that we need to pay our bills when first starting out.

Before you are able to get into a new investment you need to pick out which one you would like to go with. There ae so many different options and part of the fun is figuring out which one is the right one to match up with your skills and interest levels. If you are interested in starting your own business, you can go with that investment, but other people may be interested in working in real estate and flipping houses or renting them out. Some people want to just invest their money with a friend or family member who is starting up something, and others like to work in the different parts of the stock market. All of these have the potential of being good investments, you just need to pick one and learn how it works!

Getting started in investing is a great way to make your money work for you. There are different options and all of them are going to require you to pick out different strategies to make them work. But when you are able to do this, you can make a good income from your investment.

Chapter 5: The Different Investing Options

So, in order to be successful with investing, you need to pick out the investment opportunity that works the best for you. There are a number of options that you can pick from, but as a beginner, you will probably want to start out with just one option. Yes, there are those investors who seem to have their hands in almost every market that is out there, but this can take some time to build up and as a beginner, that is going to be way too much for you to handle. If you are still considering which type of investment you want to work with and you aren't sure where to start, check out some of these options to help make the decision easier.

The stock market

The first place that people think about when they

are working on investments is the stock market. The stock market is basically a platform where shares of companies can be bought and also sold. The shares are going to be units of ownership in the company and when you purchase one of these shares, you become one of the owners of the company. Just like a traditional owner, you will be entitled to parts of the assets as well as the future profits of the company. So if the company grows and does well, you will make an income for holding onto the shares.

A common mistake with this is that new investors assume that they should purchase as many shares as they can to make a good profit. This can be one method to make a profit, but professional investors will agree that it is best to purchase stocks that have the potential to grow. You are going to make a bigger profit from 50 shares that go up to $100 each compared to 100 shares that go up to $2 each, even if you ended up purchasing them for the same total price.

There are many options when it comes to investing in the stock market. Some people choose to pick a company to invest in for the long-term and will hold onto the stock, earning a profit each quarter as long as the company does well. Day trading is popular as well and it includes you purchasing and selling the stock all on the same day to make a bunch of little profits that add up. You can also choose from forex trading, options trading, and penny stocks as well. Each of these have their own unique set of rules and own risks so make sure that you fully understand them before starting.

The bond market

Another investment type is to work with the bond market. With this option, you are taking on less risk and you know right from the beginning how much you will earn in interest, but the return on investment is lower than the stock market or other options. In the bond market, the government and other companies are looking to borrow money from investors to expand their business or to do other things to help them grow. The investor will be able to lend out this money in the form of a band, and the company or the government can then use it for their plans.

With the bond, you will invest a certain amount of money that you are not allowed to take out again until the maturity date of the bond. Sometimes this will be a few months but it can go for several years. You will get to determine the maturity date that you are comfortable with before you start. The bond will have an interest rate attached to it, which is the amount that the investor will earn on their investment when the maturity date hits. It is a safe and secure way to make a little bit of money on your investment and can help you to grow your portfolio without all the risk that is found with some of the other options.

Investing in commodities

Some investors like to invest in commodities to see a profit. Commodities are going to refer to produce that is high in demand and also publicly traded. The products themselves will not be traded on this market. The speculators and the investors in this market are going to contract for the future value of the product. Let's look at an example of coffee. Many countries will produce coffee and this can be a great commodity to work with.

With this system, you are going to pick the commodity that you want to work with and then sign a future contract for the amount that you will spend, say $100,000. If the price of the coffee goes up by the end date, you will be able to get a profit. But if for some reason the price of the coffee goes down, you will lose the money. You need to have a good idea of the market for the commodity that you want to work with and be able to estimate what is going to happen with it in the future in order to make money with this option.

Foreign exchange

Working with foreign currencies is another option that is available for a trader. With this option, you are going to make a purchase of another currency, perhaps the GBP, when the price is relatively low compared to the American one. Then you will wait until it is worth more in the future, and change it back over to the USD, making a profit in the process. For example, if you changed over to the GBP when it was worth $1.2 USD, and then held onto it for a bit until 1 GBP was worth $1.5 USD, you would make a profit of $0.30 on every dollar that you spent, which can add up if you did a larger investment.

This was traditionally a method that was only used by the banks and governments of different countries, but it is now an option that many different people are able to use thanks to the newer technology. You do need to be careful with this option though because the currency market is always fluctuating and you never know if your money is going to be worth more or less in the future. But if you are able to hold onto the money for some time and can watch the exchange rates, you can make a good profit from this option.

Starting your own business

Some people choose to start their own business in order to start a new investment. There are many options that you can choose, from brick and mortar stores to working from home. But no matter what kind of business you decide to start, you will have to put some money forward to get started. For example, even if you want to be a writer from home, you will need to invest in a good computer, some writing software, the internet, and even some storage to help keep files in order. If you want to start a clothing store, you would need to rent out a building, purchase the clothes, hire employees, and so on.

There is quite a bit of risk that can happen with starting a business, but if you think it all out, come up with a good business plan and stick with it, you can start to make a good profit from your own business. Plus, you are able to work for yourself, instead of being stuck with a boss, so it can be very appealing to many people.

The real estate market

Many people like to work with the real estate market because this is a market that is often going up. There are some different options that you are able to use when it comes to working in the real estate market, which can make this even more popular since you get to choose the one that works for you. One option that works well with real estate is flipping houses. With this option, you will purchase a home when it is really low in price, perhaps as a foreclosure or when the market is really low. Then you will make some changes to the home, fix it up and make it look nice, and then when the market starts to go up, or when the value is higher, you will sell it to make a profit.

If you are looking to get a more continuous form of income from real estate, you can choose to purchase a home and rent it out. Your rental fees should be enough to cover the cost of the home (or the mortgage) as well as the taxes, maintenance and for you to make a little bit of income. Over time, you can add in a few different properties so that you can make a full-time income in the process.

In addition, there are a lot of options that fall into

the different categories. For example, working with rentals can include single family homes, duplexes, and apartment buildings and you can even work with commercial real estate as well. It all depends on the amount of work that you would like to put into the investment and how much money that you would like to earn.

As you can see, there are quite a few different options that you can pick from when it comes to working on an investment. All of these have the potential to bring you a lot of income, but you just need to pick out the one that meets your interests and that you will enjoy doing the most. Pick out your investment, and you are sure to see a great income in no time!

Chapter 6: The Best Investment Strategies

The next thing that you need to focus on, after you have been able to pick what kind of investment that you would like to work on, is to pick a good strategy that will help you to get this all going. There are a lot of investment types and all of them are going to work in a slightly different manner, so once you pick the investment option, you will need to look a bit more in depth to see what strategies are the most effective for you. But no matter what kind of investment you go with, there are a few strategies that will work for all of them including.

Buy low and sell high

In all of the investments that you work with, the goal is to purchase your asset at the lowest price that you can. If you purchase the investment at a price that is too high, you are going to lose out or not make very much money in the process. You are going to need to work on learning the market in order to understand when is the best time to make the purchase.

When it comes to the stock market, you will want to wait for the market to go down a bit, or at least a dip in the company that you are working with. This will allow you to purchase the stock at a lower price than usual, and then you just need to hold onto the stocks for a bit of time until the market goes up. Of course, you need to learn the difference between a stock being low priced because of the market and it being low priced because the company is failing.

You can use this in other investments as well. When it comes to working with real estate, you will want to look for a downturn in the housing market to get a good discount on the homes you want to purchase and then wait until the market goes back up and you can sell the home for a much higher price. The good news with real estate is that you can rent out the home, and make some income in the process, while you wait for the market to go back up.

No matter what kind of market you get into, you must make sure that you are purchasing the asset at the lowest price possible. This will ensure that your risks are lower and your profits higher. If you aren't good at reading the market and working on your strategy, you will find that you will purchase the asset at a high price and that it will be very difficult to sell it again without taking a loss. The lower that you can get the asset, without picking one that is already failing, the better off you will be when it comes to making a profit.

Be an expert in your market

The idea behind this strategy is that you stay inside just a few markets. You may look at the list of investing options above and feel that you should jump into all of them, but when you generalize in everything, you are setting yourself up for failure. As a beginner, you need to just stick with one option. This allows you to devote your time and energy to this, without becoming overwhelmed. Over time, as you become an expert in that market, you can expand out a little bit and try a few other options, but you should really just concentrate on one at a time and even when you expand, keep the markets similar.

For example, if you want to go into real estate, you should consider working first in renting out single family homes. Do that for a bit of time until you become comfortable with what you are doing and then you can consider expanding your portfolio to not only rent out these single-family homes but to also expand out to renting out duplexes and some small apartment buildings. You are still within the same field, but you are growing your income and diversifying your portfolio all at the same time.

If you are working in the stock market, you can take kind of the same approach. You may start out with a long-term investment in a few stocks, but then over time, you may decide to add some Forex trading or some penny stocks to the mix to help diversify and make more money. You are still working in the stock market, or something similar to it though, so you can take your knowledge and expand it out to other investments.

The thing that you need to watch out for with these investments is skipping from one to another. If you have been doing real estate, you may find that it is hard to jump over to the stock market and going from the stock market to the real estate market can be tough as well, because they are really two different types of investments. Some people have been able to do it, but it is tough and you may find that it is too much to put onto your plate. It is better to just stick with the one market, become an expert in it, and then diversify within it to see the profits that you want.

Pick out financial safe havens

After you learn a bit about how to invest into the stock market or another market for investing, you may want to learn a bit about financial safe havens. These are places where you are able to transfer your money during an economic downturn and which are less likely to be negatively impacted by the market. You would put your money over to these in order to avoid losses, at least until the economy comes back around. Ideally, your safe haven is going to be able to at least beat off inflation so you will still have the same spending power later on.

There are several different types of instruments that you can use for this, but gold is one of the most popular ones. Big investors will often move their money over to gold when the economy gets tough, and this is why you will see that the price of gold will start to climb when markets like stocks and bonds start to do poorly. Gold is not the only safe haven that you can pick. In bearish markets also see a rise in treasury bills, but gold is still the most popular because the interest rates are so low on these treasury bills.

Invest actively

If you are able to get started with a larger sum of money, you are able to start investing in an active manner in the market that you choose. In order to use this particular strategy, you must learn how to become an expert in the chosen industry and focus your energy on these in order to better learn these markets and to make some of the best decisions possible to grow your money.

For example, if you are using this type of strategy, you may want to spend some time reading up on the news of any company that you are interested in investing with. In addition, you would take some time to look at the financial statements of the company, check into their management, and find out if they are growing consistently and are actually a company that you want to work with.

There are thousands of companies who are on the stock exchange and it is important that you learn how to be an active investor. Sure, you could hand over the money to a broker and hope things go well, but the most successful investors are the ones who do the research and pick out the strategy that they want to use on their own. There is nothing wrong with talking to a broker and getting some advice, but you should never let them do all of the work for you.

Focus on the goals

Before you enter into any of the investment types, you should sit down and have some clear cut goals. You want to have a purpose behind your investing and what you want to do if you are actually successful. This will help you to create a system that will lead you to meet this goal. Some people will invest in order to make some side money to help them out with bills and other things, some want to put that money towards retirement and to help them build up a little nest egg. Others are tired of working a regular job and want to be able to work for themselves. Having these goals will help you to see that success, no matter what it is.

For example, if you are looking to make this into an investment into your retirement, you may be more likely to look for long-term investment opportunities that will help you to earn a little bit over each month. If you want to make this into a full-time income, you are going to be more interested in things like flipping homes or riding some of the big waves of the stock market so you can make this income. As you can see, these are very different options of investing, but it always depends on the goals that you are trying to reach for which one you will choose.

So before you decide to go and purchase your asset or get into your chosen market, you need to sit down and decide what your goals are going to be for that investment. Then you can write down the plan that you want to follow in order to make these goals a reality. It is nice to have dreams and to hope that the investment asset that you choose will help you to get there, but if you don't plan ahead and make sure that you have the right strategy, you are never going to see the results that you want.

It is so much you are able to do when it comes to picking out an investment and seeing it grow. Picking out a good strategy will help you to really see the success that you are looking for because it leads you to pick the right asset and making decisions that will make you successful. No matter what kind of investment you choose to go with, make sure to follow some of these simple strategies and you are sure to see some of the success that you are looking for.

PART 2

CHAPTER 1: UNDERSTANDING OPTIONS TRADING

Options trading, also known as *binary options trading,* is just like forex and stock trading. However, you do not need to buy currencies or stocks. Instead, you simply predict whether the value of an underlying asset will increase or decrease at a specified time. It is this simplicity of options trading that attract so many investors. It is an option contract that has a fixed payout.

Options trading vs. forex and stock trading

In forex and stocking trading, you buy currencies or stocks and sell them for profit. In options trading, you do not need to buy any trading asset. You only predict whether the price of an underlying asset will be higher or lower than its current price at the expiration date. Also, in forex and stock trading, your profit will depend on the increase in the value of a particular currency or stock that you have purchased. In options trading, the potential profit is fixed and is revealed to you even before you commence a trade.

It is not uncommon for forex and stock traders to wait for weeks and months just to see a little profit from their investment. Many times, they even lose their investment without any chance of getting any profit. This happens when the price of their stocks or currency drops. With options trading, there is always a potential to earn a big amount of profit even when the price of an underlying asset decreases. You do not have to wait for weeks or months; you can double, or even triple, your investment in a few minutes.

Options trading vs. gambling

There are similarities between options trading and gambling. In some jurisdictions, options trading is literally considered gambling. Just like the casino game called *baccarat* where you decide whether the winning hand is *banker* or *player*, in options trading, you will decide whether the value of an underlying asset will rise (Call) or fall (Put) at the expiration time. Just like the table games in the casino, there is a fixed payout for a favorable outcome.

You might be wondering, "Is options trading gambling?" It depends. If you do options trading by relying on guesswork and pure luck, then you are gambling. However, if you consider every wager that you make an investment decision and take the serious effort to study the market and research the different underlying assets being traded, then you are an investor or trader.

It does not really matter whether you see yourself as a gambler or a trader. In the end, what matters is how much profit you have made, if any.

The Basics

Let us move on to the specific parts of options trading. Do not worry; options trading is very easy. You can learn the basics in less than five minutes. It is only like speculating the outcome of a coin flip.

Call vs. Put

There are only two main options to choose from. In options trading, you just have to know whether the outcome will be a *Call* or a *Put*. Simple, right?

Choose the Call option if you predict that the price of an underlying asset will be *above* its current price at the expiration date.

Choose the Put option if you predict that the price of an underlying asset will be *below* its current price at the expiration date.

These two terms are referred to by many names, depending on the trading platform that you use. They are also known as Up/Down, Above/Below, Rise/Fall, and others.

Strike price

This refers to the price at which an asset can be bought or sold at a certain time. In options trading, this simply refers to the Call or Put option. The Call option is the value at which the underlying asset can be bought, while the Put option is when it can be sold at a specified time.

Expiration time

The expiration time, or simply expiry time, signifies the end of a trading period. This is also the time when you can determine whether or not you have made the right investment decision. Therefore, this is the moment when you will experience a profit or a loss.

In-the-money vs. out-the-money

In-the-money is a *win*. It means that you have made

the right investment decision and earned a profit. On the contrary, out-the-money means that you have lost your wager.

Long-term option

In options trading, you get to choose how long a trade will last (expiration date). A long-term option simply refers to a trade that is long as 24 hours or more. A long-term option can last for a day, weeks, and months.

Speed option

As the name already implies, speed options are trades that last for a short period of time. This can be as fast as 30 seconds, a minute, or up to five to fifteen minutes, depending on the platform that you use.

Assets

Assets are valuable financial instruments. In options trading, you do not have to purchase any asset, you just have to determine if the value of an asset will be greater than or lower than its current price at the expiration time.

When trading binary options, the following assets are traded:

- stocks
- index
- commodities
- currency pairs

Bear market vs. bull market

On the one hand, a bear market means that the prices of certain assets are decreasing or are about to decrease. On the other hand, a bull market means that the prices of certain assets are increasing or are about to increase.

Take note, however, that even though a bear market is considered a negative sentiment, it does not affect you as a trader. In fact, you can even profit from it. This is because options trading has a dual nature: You can make a good amount of profit whether the price of certain underlying assets increase or decrease, provided you choose the right option (Call vs. Put).

Brokers and trading platforms

Before you can start trading binary options, you need to open an account with a broker. You can find many brokers when you make a search online. However, you need to choose a broker that will best suite your needs. Unfortunately, there are also scammers out there, so it is best to work only with a broker that has a well-established reputation.

Here is a list of trusted brokers. Take note that trading platforms may change their policies and management team. Therefore, even the most trusted brokers may no longer be a good choice tomorrow. Before you open an account, check the latest ratings and reviews given by other traders.

- iq option (www.iqoption.com)
- OptionRobot (www.optionrobot.com)
- Automated   Binary (www.automatedbinary.com)
- Finpari (www.finpari.com)
- 24option (www.24option.com)
- fortuneJack (www.fortunejack.com) *bitcoin casino with binary options*

Important note:

Be sure to check the *banking options*. Many brokers accept many methods to make a deposit but only have limited options for making a withdrawal.

CHAPTER 2: RISKS & BENEFITS

Like any business venture, there are a number of risks and benefits associated with options trading. Here are the things that you can expect:

Market risk

The market is composed of real people. This is why it is extremely volatile. And, although there are methods that have been developed to predict market movements, there is no guaranteed way to determine how the market responds.

Lack of ownership

In options trading, you only wager on the future valuation of an underlying asset. Therefore, you do not exercise any right of ownership over any stock or asset.

High-risk investment

Like any other business that offers a high reward, the risk involved is also high. Unlike in trading stocks where you get to keep a losing stock with an opportunity that its price will soon increase or at least sell the stock to cut down your losses, you do not get to keep anything if you encounter a loss in options trading. In options trading, when you lose a trade, you lose the whole amount that you wager on that particular trade.

Limited opportunity

In options trading, the potential payout is already fixed even before you commence a trade. You cannot get a profit higher than the fixed payout. In forex or stock trading, the potential profit is almost limitless.

No liquidity

There is no liquidity because you do not have ownership of the stock or asset being traded. When you commence a trade, you just have to wait for the trading period to end and hope for the best. However, liquidity should not be an issue. After all, there are trades that can last for just a day, even less.

Losing is normal

Although there are people who rake in serious profits with options trading, the majority of traders lose their money, and they lose it within a short period of time.

If your entrepreneurial spirit remains strong and convinced despite the risks that you will encounter along your journey, then it is time for you to know the notable benefits of options trading.

The Benefits

High Return

For those who engage in forex or stock trading, a 50% is already considered high. And, usually, they would have to wait for months just to get a 50% profit. Most of the time, they do not even reach 50%. With options trading, getting a 90% per trade is normal. You can double your money in less than an hour.

Simplicity

It is the beautiful simplicity of options trading that makes it very attractive. You do not need to have any trading portfolio or any gambling experience. You can learn and start earning money with options trading almost instantly.

Fixed payout

Unlike other investment opportunities where you do not know how much money you can make, options trading lets you know the exact amount that you can profit before you commence a trade.

Quick turnover rate

Options trading allows you to choose just how long you want a trade to last. With speed trading, you can make multiple trades in less than five minutes.

Asset variety

Since you do not have to purchase any asset or currency, you have all the available underlying assets to choose from. Also, the minimum amount per trade is usually low, so you can easily diversify the assets that you invest in.

Controlled risk

You do not have to worry about hidden charges or surcharges. Whatever amount that you spend for a particular trade is your total risk. If you just want to risk $100, then simply invest $100, and there is nothing else that you should worry about.

Instant trading

Most established brokers offer a mobile phone feature. This will allow you to manage your account and commence a trade anytime and anywhere.

CHAPTER 3: STRATEGIES

Most people who lose their money with options trading either have no strategy at all and just rely on pure luck, or have a poor and underdeveloped strategy. If you want to rake in serious profits with options trading, you need to have a solid strategy. Unlike casino games where you simply have to vary the amount of your bets, success in options trading requires serious research, analysis, and practice.

Fundamental analysis

Fundamental analysis is considered the lifeblood of investment. This is the key to increasing your chances of making a profit. Remember that the market is run by real people and businesses, In fundamental analysis, you need to gather various information and analyze the economy, financial statements of businesses, as well as the latest news, among others. By analyzing these data, you can come up with a better investment decision. For example, if there is a report that the problem of the high unemployment rate has just been resolved in the U.S., and all other things being normal, then you can expect the value of the U.S. currency to increase.

If you like numbers, then fundamental analysis is the way to go. However, it is not recommended for speed options. This is because economic and business changes take time. It is best to use this method for trades that last for more than 12 hours.

Technical analysis

If you do not like analyzing lots of numbers, then technical analysis may be for you. Technical analysis is more visual. You will be analyzing charts and graphs. Technical analysis is excellent for fast trading or speed options. The proper way to use this method is to view the available graphs and look for patterns.

A note about patterns: Patterns depend on the latest trend. Is it a bull or a bear market? The risk here is that trends are not permanent. They change —and they usually change quickly. The key here is to find a pattern and be able to place your wager just before the trend changes.

Algorithmic and signals

By using computer programs and apps that can be installed on your computer, you will know where to invest in. This is an easy and quick way to come up with a decision; however, this method is not recommended because it is unreliable. There is simply no computer program that can accurately read the market's movement. However, this can be useful as secondary information.

Co-integration trading

This strategy uses the correlation that is created between two underlying assets. This usually occurs when two assets are in the same industry or have the same market. Due to their high correlation, you will notice that their prices are always close to each other. Hence, when a sudden significant gap appears between their prices, there is the highest probability that their prices will soon be close to each other again. So, you either place a Call option on the stock whose value has dropped or a Put option on the stock with a higher price.

Aggressive betting

As the name already implies, it is aggressive when you wager a big percentage of your total investment per trade, like wagering 20% per trade. Of course, the most aggressive way is to wager your whole investment on a single trade, but such is not recommended.

A famous aggressive betting strategy that is widely used by gamblers is known as the Martingale. This is where you double your wager after every loss. For example, first, you wager $10. If you lose the trade, you then wager $20. If you lose the trade again, you next wager $40, and so on... until you win a trade. When you win a trade, you go back to your initial wager of $10.

Although the Martingale looks feasible and reasonable, it is not effective in the long run.

Unfortunately, it is not surprising to experience a series of wrong investment decisions. If you get really unlucky, you may even make 10 wrong decisions in a row. There only use this strategy for a short term, and be sure to back it up with sufficient research.

Conservative betting

Your betting strategy is considered conservative if you only use a small percentage of your total investment per trade, preferably just around 1%-3%. This is good if you already have a well-developed strategy that has a high rate of success.

Corrective

This is a good strategy to use when you see a sudden and significant increase or decrease in price, especially when such price spike is not clearly justified by existing factors. In such a case, you can expect for the price to balance out by reverting to its original value prior to the price spike, or somewhat close to it.

Breakout

This strategy works well with currency pairs. When a currency pair follows a tight or close price difference, and if you see them break out, the probability is high that their prices will continue to breakout. Although they will most likely revert to their normal price range, such will take time.

Asset mastery

Pick any underlying asset of your choice. Now, find out everything that you can about your chosen asset. Follow on the news and gather as much data as you can about that asset. Do this on a regular basis, preferably daily. You will notice that the more you know about a particular asset, the better predictions you can make. This also confirms that the market does not move at random.

CHAPTER 4: KEYS TO SUCCESS

Regardless whether you only want to trade for profit or for fun, you should know the best practices that can help increase your chances of success and minimize your losses.

Money management

No matter how well developed your strategy is or how much you have increased your success rate, you can lose your investment if you fail to manage your money properly. Also, do not use the money that you need to cover your household bills and other obligations. Do not forget that options trading is a high-risk investment.

Cash out

An important part of money management is learning to cash out. Unfortunately, many traders do not cash out their profits. Although it is good to grow your funds, you should still cash out from time to time. Take note that your profits only become real when you turn them into real cash; otherwise, they are nothing but numbers on a screen and almost have no difference with demo credits. Therefore, always cash out, you do not have to cash out everything, if you want, you can just cash out 20% of your profits on a regular basis.

Research and analysis

The possibility of doing a research and analysis is what separates options trading from gambling. You need to research and be updated on the news about the businesses themselves, as well as the factors that affect business performance. When analyzing, you need to drop your personal preferences and see everything as they are. Your investment decision must be based on facts without any bias. Research is key. Remember that the outcome of every trade and the movements of the graphs are mere reflections of reality. The more you know about the economy, real people, and real businesses, the better you can make an investment decision.

Focus on the assets

Although the graphs and charts may reveal to you certain patterns, it is worth noting that such patterns are not always present. And, many times, they do not stay for so long. After all, trends are meant to change, considering that the market is alive and continues to move. When making an investment decision, be sure that you have good information on the asset that is the subject of your trade. It must be emphasized that the more you know about a particular asset, the higher is the probability of making the right investment decision.

The importance of keeping a journal

Although having a journal is not a requirement, writing a trading journal can be very helpful. You do not need to be a professional writer; you only need to be open and honest when you write your journal.

A journal will allow you to think outside the box and be a better trader. You can write anything in your journal. You can write about your new learnings, mistakes, or any adjustments that you make to your strategy. Should you decide to use a journal, be sure to update it regularly

Start small

It can be very tempting to invest a lot in a particular trade when you know that you have researched a great deal just to make that trade. However, if you are a beginner, it is best to start small and focus on increasing your success rate. First, you need to get a feel of options trading and develop your strategy. If it is your first time to trade, do not focus on making money right away. After all, once you have enough experience and confidence, you can easily increase the amount that you invest per trade. To have a good and steady profit, aim to have a success rate of at least 60%-70%.

Focus on the numbers

There are ways to somehow manipulate the stocks for a short period of time. Especially these days when you can easily and quickly send a message to the world with just a few clicks of a mouse, some people are able to make their stocks look more attractive than they really are. Unfortunately, even the media may have its own preferences and prejudices. And many so-called "experts" on options trading cannot be trusted. Therefore, you need to focus on the numbers. Words are easy to manipulate and misinterpret, but numbers do not lie. When numbers are unduly manipulated, such fraudulent scheme tends to be obvious.

Do not chase after your losses

When you engage in options trading, you should be prepared to encounter some losses. You cannot expect to make the right investment decisions all the time. Losses are part of this kind of investment. The important thing is that the outcome of all your trades results in a positive profit.

Never chase after your losses. If you do, there is a higher risk of losing more money. Instead, be positive and focus on your profits, and how to profit some more.

Most people chase after their losses by increasing the amount of their wager per trade. This is risky because your strategy may not be suited for an aggressive betting, and your funds may not be enough to handle such big wagers.

Develop your strategy

In options trading, developing a strategy simply does not end. This is because you are dealing with a living and continuously evolving market. Therefore, you should continuously work on your strategy. It must be flexible enough to adapt to market changes and effective enough to make a decent amount of profit.

Have your own understanding of the market

True experts do not have the same strategy or share the same viewpoints all the time. They are experts because they have developed their own understanding of the market, and they can justify their views no matter how odd they may be. In the same manner, you also need to develop your own understanding of options trading and the market. In the beginning, you can rely on expert tips and advice, but soon you need to have your own way of making an investment decision. After all, nobody can get rich just by relying on expert advice. Also, out of the many people out there who claim to be "experts," only a few of them are true experts. Most of these "experts" have more losses than profits.

Practice

The only way to truly learn options trading is by actual practice. It is experience that will make you a real binary options trader. Take note that practicing does not only mean making a series of trades. In options trading, placing a trade is the easiest part. True practice means doing research and studying the various underlying assets, businesses, as well as the market behavior, among others.

PART 3

Chapter One: Locating the Best Houses to Flip

When you flip a house, you are going to be buying a house below the market price and then fixing what needs to be fixed before you turn around and sell it for what you hope is going to be a profit. But, before you can buy the house, you need to know how you are going to find the perfect property to flip.

Step one: Search through the Multiple Listing Service. The MLS is going to be a database that you can look through to find houses that are for sale by a broker. If you are using a realtor to help you find houses to buy and flip, then you are going to have the option to get them to assist you in looking through the MLS in a more advanced search so that you can find the perfect house to flip. The MLS offers a search option that will show you all of the foreclosures that are in your area so that you can buy them for a lower price than the other properties that you find on the MLS.

Step two: Join a real estate group. With a real estate group, you are going to be placed in the middle of the realtors in your area, and you are going to be able to get some advice on what you plan on doing next so that you can see if it is worth spending the money or not. With a real estate group, there is the possibility that you are going to hear about investors that want to offload a property due to the fact that they do not have the time needed to flip it or are wanting to pull their money out of it. It is opportunities like this that are going to get you some good properties that you can flip.

Step three: another way that you can get property without paying a lot of money is to pay attention to the tax auctions and the sales that your local sheriff's office have. However, you need to be careful when you are buying properties from these sources due to the fact that you never know about the price. That is why you should ensure that you know the price of the property before you close on it so that you are not having to pay more money than what you discussed when buying it.

In buying a property off of unpaid taxes, you are going to be responsible for catching the taxes up on the property before it is yours.

At a tax auction or sheriff's sale, you will need to register yourself as a bidder due to the fact that the sale is open to the public and anyone can bid on the property and get it. It is a good idea to talk to the attorney that is representing the bank for that auction so you can get a feel for what they are looking to get out of that property.

You always have the option of finding houses in a more traditional way as well such as looking through your local newspaper, contacting people who have inherited houses but may not be wanting to live there, or houses that are owned but sitting empty due to the owner living somewhere else.

Chapter Two: House Flipping

House flipping may sound like a quick way for you to make a profit, but there are things that you need to know before you can begin to flip houses and actually make a profit.

Step one: Make sure you commit to the flip. You do not want to just buy a house because you are excited about it but not seeing it through. It is important to know that flipping houses is not a hobby, but a business that you are getting yourself into. So, before you get into house flipping, evaluate your goals and see if you are going to be committed to the flip before you start.

Step two: Get the proper education. You do not have to learn everything about flipping houses before you start, but you do need to know the basics. Flipping houses is going to be an experience where you learn as you go. Therefore, knowing the basics is going to give you the boost you need to ensure that you are not going into the flip with no clue of what has to be done or where you should start. One of the best methods to learn something is to teach it, so once you have learned the basics, start trying to teach someone in your life; even if that person is your cat! The action of speaking about what it is that you learned will help you to remember it better.

Step three: Know the math of flipping houses. If you do not know the proper math, then you are not going to know if you are getting a good deal out of the house or not. Do not depend on a calculator to do all of the math for you. You should do the math by hand as well so that you can understand where the numbers that the calculator came up with came from.

Step four: Market research. Just like we discussed in the first chapter, you need to find the best resources that are going to show you where you should locate a house and get it for the best price. You do not want to spend a lot of money on a house that you could end up losing money on in the long run.

Step five: Evaluate your flip budget. How do you plan on paying for all of the supplies and labor that is going to be needed for your flip? There are a few methods that most house flippers use when paying for their flip that you can use if it is the best method for you.

- Cash: this is the simplest solution because you are not going to have to worry about not having the money. However, you are going to have to worry about having the money in your account before you can begin.

- Conventional financing: with a bank loan, you can use the money to flip the house, but you are going to have to be careful with this because some banks are not going to lend the money if the home is not finished.

- Home equity loan: this method is only going to work if you have a large amount of equity that is in your personal home.

- Hard money lender: the hard money donor is going to be a company or an individual that lends money to something that is considered to be high risk. But, they are going to charge high fees and high interest rates in order to get the money back. Ideally, you are going to want to stick to this type of funding because your only going to have about a year maturity date on the loan.

- Private money: in the event that you know someone who would loan you the money to do your flip, then you are going to want to talk to them about the interest rate that they were going to charge you if they loaned you the money. But, you are going to discover that this is one of the cheapest sources that you are going to find.

- Combination: you can also mix and match the methods that were discussed above to get the money that you need. You may find that you end up owing several people money, but if you owe several people small amounts of money, that is going to be better than owing them a large amount that has a high interest rate on it.

Chapter Three:

Things You Need for Flipping a House

It is easy to believe that when you buy a house to flip all you are going to have to do is buy the house, repaint it and plant some bushes before you turn around and resell it for a profit. But, if it was that simple, then why aren't more people doing it? That is because you have to have a specific set of skills to be able to take a home and flip it. If you do not have the skills that are needed to get what has to be done, done, then you need to know someone who does or hire someone who can do the job for you.

1. The initial thing that you need is a group of experts. It does not hurt to have someone who

knows the legal aspects of flipping a house, someone who is good with accounting, and someone who can do the construction. If you are able to do some of this, then you are going to be able to save more money. But, you are not going to be equipped to do it all because you are most likely trying to work against a clock and on a tight budget to get the house flipped so that you can hopefully collect a profit. It does not hurt also to have a real estate agent, insurance agent, and a home inspector so that you are not opening yourself up for a lawsuit later on down the road in case someone gets hurt while the house is being renovated or catches fire after you sell it.

2. Someone who is good at home improvement or be a handyman. If you look at people who flip houses, they are typically people who like to work with their hands because they can step

in and do some of the work themselves if the time limit on fixing up the house begins to get too close. Being handy is great for a flipper because they are going to be able to do the work themselves which is going to save money on getting someone else to do it. This also works out well when it is impossible to get out someone who is certified to do that job out to the house to do it inside of the time limit that you are working on.

3. You need to know the area that you are buying the house. This is important because knowing more about the area and the prices of the houses around the one you are looking to purchase will tell you about what you are going to be able to get out of it. But, it will also be valuable to know any future developments the area may experience.

4. Before you buy the house, take someone in who is a good estimator. Have them look at the house and tell you about what it is going to cost to fix the house up and what they think that you are going to be able to get out of it once you do fix it up so that you can know if it is worth the risk or if you should move on to another house. If you underestimate the cost that it is going to take to fix up the house, then you may end up finding that you will lose money.

5. Have patience. When you first get started flipping houses, you may end up losing money. But, with some patience and learning from your mistakes will help you to not lose money anymore and you are going to be able to flip houses like a pro. Just do not expect it to work overnight, like anything, it is going to take

time for you to learn the art of flipping houses

fully.

Chapter Four:

Mistakes to Avoid when Flipping Houses

Whenever people rush to get into flipping houses, they tend to make the type of mistakes that cost them money due to the fact that they do not look at the basics. You are not going to want to make the same mistakes that those who have come before you have made, so in this chapter, we are going to tell you some of the mistakes that you are going to want to avoid when flipping houses.

1. Not enough money. Getting into real estate is going to be expensive, and the first expense that you are going to come across is the cost of buying the property. You hear about no

down or a low down payment, but it is easier to say you will find a vendor that will actually stick to this deal than it is to find one. You need to make sure that you do your research on the financial options that are available to you before you choose one so that you are not going with the first one that comes across your path. One of the best ways to calculate the total cost of the property that you may be buying is to use a mortgage calculator that way you can put the interest rates in from various vendors before you decide on which one is going to be best for you. If possible, paying in cash is going to eliminate any interest cost that you are going to come across, but then you will need to pay the property taxes and utilities. On top of all of that, you are going to have the renovation costs. If you do not factor everything in, then you are going to end up underestimating your budget and losing money.

2. Not enough time. Whenever you get into the business of flipping houses, you are going to want to make sure that you set everything up on a schedule and that is going to take up a great majority of your time so that you are not holding onto the house for too long. Not to mention you are going to have to schedule things such as inspections and in order to get the house inspected you have to have all of your renovations done before the inspector comes out. Then, if you are the one who is showing the house to prospective buyers, you are going to have to be there each time that someone wants to see the house. So, flipping houses is not going to just be something that you can do in your spare time; it is something that is going require you to make a

commitment to spending time doing what needs to be done.

3. Not enough skill. Most of the money that you are going to get from flipping houses is going to come from sweat equity. If you are able to do something such a hang drywall or install plumbing, then you are going to have some of the skill that is required to do some of the work on renovating your house. The more you can do, the less money you will need to spend on hiring professionals to do the work.

4. Not enough knowledge. As discussed earlier you need to know the basics of flipping a house before you get into it. If you do not at least know what it is that you need to do in order to get started on flipping a house, you will be going into it blindly, and that is going to cause you to lose money due to the fact you

are going to get frustrated and give up on the flip.

5. Not enough patience. If you expect the house to be flipped overnight or you are a person who does not have a lot of patience, to begin with, then flipping houses is not for you. Flipping houses takes time and patience and depending on how bad the house is that you buy is going to depend on how much work needs to be done. You need to have the patience that is required to get the work done properly so that the house will pass inspection. On top of that, you need to make sure you are being patient with those that are helping you out with the renovations because sometimes there are unexpected problems that you are going to run into that will require you to find a solution which could end up taking more time than you expected.

PART 4

INTRODUCTION

Before we get into the different types of passive income, let's first talk about what it actually is. Passive income is money that is earned from a source in which he or she is not physically involved. Like active income, passive income is taxed, though it is usually treated a little differently by the Internal Revenue Service (IRS). States differ slightly in their tax laws, so make sure to see a certified public accountant before filing your taxes with the IRS.

Overall, there are three types of income. Passive, which is the subject of this e-book, active and portfolio income. To give a little insight into the difference between the three, we will briefly outline active and portfolio income before delving into different types of passive income.

Although it should seem self-explanatory, we are going to detail what active income is. Active income is a job that requires the earner to be physically present. In the United States, the most common forms of active income are hourly and salary. Hourly employees earn a wage for each hour they work while salary employees are paid a flat rate regardless of how many hours they put in. Most companies pay weekly or biweekly, although there are a few who pay monthly. However, those tend to be government or teaching positions.

Surprisingly enough, freelance work is also considered active income. The person in the freelance position gets paid for work upon its completion. One of the downfalls of freelance work is if you are sick or unable to complete a project, there is no paycheck. Writing articles, e-books and traditional books and photography are the most common types of freelance jobs.

Portfolio income is money earned from royalties, investments, capital gains and dividends. For tax purposes, the IRS does not consider portfolio income to be passive income as it does not come from traditional businesses or passive investments.

Now that we have talked about the different types of income let's talk about why passive income is a great way to earn extra money for savings, retirement, vacations or anything else you would like to spend your money on.

While you should be very excited about what we will learn in this book, it is important to note that passive income does not mean 'easy money.' Like all other forms of income, there is some work involved whether it is research, development, writing an e-book or selling photographs online. Wouldn't turning a hobby into income be an excellent way to earn some extra money? One of the ways we will discuss in this book is exactly that. Even using a hobby to earn a passive income takes some time and effort up front, although it is probably the most enjoyable of all the forms of passive income, we will cover in this book.

If you have some time and energy to devote to passive income from the comfort of your own home (maybe even in your pajamas while you sip coffee), let's talk about some of the exciting ways you can earn a passive income!

Chapter 1

Surveys, Selling Photos

& Teaching Classes

Surprisingly enough, there are lots of ways to make money on the internet. We will list some of the more passive ways to earn money online and then give you some insight into how you can get going with passive income online.

Websites like InboxDollars actually pay people to shop online, play games and even search the web. InboxDollars has been around since 2000, and the company itself employs thirty people. They offer anywhere between 1-10 cents per email read and the payment on playing games or going to an affiliate website varies. As with any web-based income potential, there are pros and cons to InboxDollars. The first payment isn't sent until you've earned thirty bucks. At that, it can take up to two weeks to receive payment so if you are looking for quick and easy, InboxDollars isn't the place to be. However, if you are hanging out in front of a computer while sipping on a latte at your local coffee shop, why not sign up and earn some money simply for surfing the net or reading emails? You are already online anyway, right?

Another site similar to InboxDollars is called **SwagBucks.** InboxDollars website is a little easier to maneuver, and they categorize each option for earning cash online. SwagBucks does require you to sign up with them before you can see the earning potential. Swagbucks doesn't pay in cold, hard cash. They pay in the form of "SwagBucks," which is their term for earning points. Each SwagBuck is approximately one cent. That means once you've accrued one-hundred, you've made roughly one dollar. SwagBucks are redeemable for gift cards only. There are no checks or payments sent to your PayPal account. As opposed to InboxDollars, SwagBucks will actually pay you for referrals, in the form of their SwagBucks, of course. For every survey your referral completes, you get ten percent. That's actually a great deal considering it is someone else doing the work, right? One last thing to mention about these websites. They both pay you to sign up for trial offers, which is something you need to be very careful with. While they both will pay a pretty decent amount for your signing up, you have to remember to cancel your membership within the month, or your credit card will be charged for the service. Of the two, Swagbucks pays more; usually enough to earn a twenty-five dollar gift card, which is actually a fantastic deal!

In addition to earning a passive income by signing up for websites like those mentioned previously, you can also sell your photography online. Obviously, this is geared toward those who enjoy taking photos as a hobby. As it isn't for everyone, we will discuss it briefly before moving onto the next subject.

If you do enjoy taking photos of scenic overlooks, nature, or even people (with their permission of course), you can sell your photos to places like Shutterstock and Stock photo. Depending on which site you choose, they will pay either with a percentage of overall sales of your photo or a flat fee for each photo that is sold to the client. One of the great things about selling your photos is one picture can earn money more than once. Each time it is sold, you'll get a percentage (or the aforementioned flat fee). If you always liked photography but hadn't really given it a second thought, maybe now is the time to do so. You do have to go out and take the pictures, but it is a great way to get some exercise, fresh air, see some awesome sights and earning some of that passive income!

Another way to earn passive income is to write an e-book. Like photography, it has to be something that you have an interest in. Since it isn't everyone's cup of tea, we'll go over it briefly, just like we did with photography.

There are several ways to make money with writing e-books. Fiction, fantasy, how-to, cookbooks...the list is endless. There is some work up front, and if you aren't the best with commas and periods, it might be prudent to hire an editor just to make sure you don't miss anything major. Some of the most popular books are how to and fantasy. If you are particularly knowledgeable on a subject, or you have an incredibly active imagination, either of those would be an excellent way to start earning passive income.

Once the book is written, you can publish it on Amazon and wait for some money to start coming in. If you want to make decent money, you will want to invest some time in marketing. This is something you can do yourself using your already established social media outlets. Facebook, Twitter, and Instagram are great for free advertising.

Did you know that you can make money by posting YouTube videos online? This too takes some work and a bit of marketing on your part, but once you get going who knows? Maybe you will be the next YouTube sensation! As we outlined with writing an e-book, there are several areas in which you can create a YouTube channel. Book or restaurant reviews, music, opinions, comedy, music and tutorials of all kinds including hair, makeup, rebuilding engines or fixing just about anything around the house. From sinks to refrigerators, people are always looking for a way to fix things themselves so that they don't have to spend thousands of dollars hiring someone to come out to their house and take care of it for them. The key to success with this type of internet income is marketing. We already talked about those social media outlets in the e-book section. You can utilize those to market your YouTube videos as well. Making the video itself is not as easy as it sounds, but it can be quite a bit of fun. There will be some trial and error, and once it's done there will be some editing involved, but it is free to post videos to YouTube meaning no upfront cost. You'll only need to put the time and energy into creating your YouTube masterpiece.

The last topic we'll go over for internet income is creating an online course or an online guide. Is there something that you are particularly great at? Perhaps you know a lot about medieval history, how to rebuild a transmission for a particular or rare car, or maybe you can teach people how to sell real estate. Really, whatever you are good at and/or passionate about, you can create a course to help others who might be looking to expand their own knowledge base.

While there are a few platforms in which you can do this, one of the best-known platforms is Udemy.com. They have over *eight million* students looking to learn something new every day. That is a huge number of people to whom you can sell your product. What's great about this is there isn't a whole lot you need to do in the way of marketing. Udemy has it all categorized. You would want to write a killer description of your tutorial, though. That way, you would have a bit of an advantage over others who might be teaching related online courses. This is literally something you can make money at while you sleep. Your course can include a video, tutorials, lessons and checklists. What's great about Udemy is you can make it your own. There are even several price points for this website meaning you can have a higher price point that has all the bells and whistles and then lower price points that have a little less, but still the same great information you are providing at the higher price. This makes it so you can market to a larger group of people maximizing your potential for passive income.

Finally, you can make an online guide. Again, the possibilities here are endless. You can create a guide to the best fishing in the country, white water rafting, skiing...whatever you'd like. Online guides don't usually cost anything to the person searching for those items.

Where you make your money with guides is through advertisers. If you are creating a guide to fishing, you'd want to check with bait shops and any outdoorsy type retail place that would want to place an ad on your site. Some pay by the click, others pay if someone purchases something through their website after clicking from your guide. It depends on the retailer, but this is a great way to earn passive income. What's not to love about sharing your expertise and making money in the process?

We've covered quite a few things in this opening chapter! We have outlined just a few of the ways you can earn a passive income using the internet. One of the best things about the things we talked about is they can be fun, especially if writing or photography is a hobby. Taking surveys probably isn't how you picture yourself spending your weekend, but when it comes to passive income, you have to admit that clicking through a survey or getting paid to play a new online game is pretty passive. That being said, there are much more ways and exploring those is just a Google search away. Find something that interests you and the sky is the limit.

Chapter 2 – Passive Income Earned From Investing

Investing may sound daunting. It's highly likely you are looking to passive income as a way to make money because you don't have a lot of excess cash laying around. Let's face it...the majority of us don't. While investing may sound intimidating and expensive, rest assured there are ways to earn a passive income without having to put a second mortgage on your house or dip into your children's college funds.

One of the first things you can look at in the way of investing is joining a Lending Club. This is a web-based lending program geared toward peer to peer borrowing and lending. Unlike traditional investing in US Treasury Securities or bank certificates, Lending Clubs offer a much higher yield on returns. Bonds and other bank certificates usually earn about one-percent which is passive income in the basest of terms. Making that little every year won't do much in the way of helping you retire sooner or get to that beach house you've been looking to vacation at for the past few years. Lending Clubs have a much higher interest rate and with that comes an increased risk. Like bank loans, those given through a Lending Club are at risk of default meaning if the borrower doesn't repay the note to you, that's money you've just lost on investment.

The risk of a defaulted loan is minimal if you know what kinds of loans are more likely to be paid back. For example, you wouldn't want to invest in a mom and pop coffee shop that is slotted for location in the midst of several big chain coffee shops. While that is a risk that can pay off, it might be a little too risky for your liking. And that's okay! When it comes to investing, you have to do what makes you comfortable. Especially when we are talking about putting up some of your own, hard-earned money. Remember, the thought of doing that might make you a little uneasy, but the payoff can be very rewarding.

Lending Clubs usually recommend you start out with an initial deposit of around 2500.00. You can invest as little as twenty-five dollars on a single loan, meaning you can actually invest in up to one-hundred businesses at a time. The potential for earning passive income using this method is higher, and you are invested in businesses that you didn't have to put all your blood, sweat and tears into starting up. That's pretty passive and far less stressful.

The beautiful thing about Lending Clubs is there are several that are free to join. That's great if you know a good chunk of what you do have saved is going to go to the initial deposit.

In terms of investing, you can also look into Index Funds. It is a form of mutual fund that helps you to invest in the stock market in an entirely passive manner. These is especially great because you don't have to concern yourself with choosing an investment, knowing when to buy or sell, or rebalancing your portfolio. All of those things are handled by the index fund.

One of the best sites to set up an index fund is Scottrade. Their website is easy to maneuver, setting up an account is pretty affordable. Their website offers levels of investment and depending on how much you invest; you'll also be rewarded with a minimum of fifty free trades. It's a pretty awesome deal. Not to mention, you get to choose where your money goes. Also, if you set up with Scottrade and decide to invest in a different manner, you'll already have an account established with them. Along the same lines as investing, if you are looking to get a retirement fund going (outside of a traditional 401k you may have through your full-time job), Roth IRA's are a great place to put your money. And, if you leave your job you can roll your 401k into a Roth IRA without having to pay huge tax penalties.

Another way to invest online is the use of a Robo-advisor. If you are worried about trying to decipher stocks and how the market works, let a Robo-advisor do the job for you. One Robo-advisor that gets some of the best reviews is Betterment. You provide them with the funds, and their algorithms will find the best investments for you. In addition to that, it will keep your portfolio balanced. Talk about passive! While there is the upfront cost of investing, you won't have to stress over reading the paper or watching the news every day to see where your stocks are at.

One of the most well-known and popular ways of investing is in the Real Estate Market. As with most investments, this can come with some risk, and there are more ways to invest in Real Estate than just flipping houses or turning them into rental properties. Because rental properties are the most common, we will discuss them in a little greater detail.

Real Estate rentals aren't entirely passive income makers. There is some work involved in finding the house or apartment complex, but once you've found a property and rented it out, you'll only need to make sure your tenant sends you a rent check every month. You can also hire property management companies to manage your rental for you. Their typical fee is approximately ten-percent of the rental amount every month. One of the benefits of rental properties is once the original loan is paid off, your earnings go up substantially. If you have more than one property that's paid off and bringing in decent rent each month, you might even be able to retire and turn your investments into full-fledged passive income.

Along the same lines, you can also invest in Real Estate Investment Trusts, also known as REITs. As previously mentioned, investing in real estate itself isn't entirely passive. However, if you want to invest in real estate completely passively, REITs are the way to go. This is kind of like investing in a mutual fund with various real estate projects as opposed to stocks or bonds. Like mutual funds, REITs are managed by professionals, so you won't have to worry about learning all the legalities of real estate. REITs pay a higher dividend than most bonds, stocks or even bank investments. You can also sell your REIT at any time making it a more fluid form of passive income since you'll never actually have to invest in an actual property.

There is one final note we'll mention in regards to real estate. If you already own your own home and have some space available, you can rent out that unused space on Airbnb. It's a relatively new concept, but over the past year, it has exploded all around the globe. This engine allows people to travel all over the world and stay places much cheaper than hotels, hostels or traditional bed and breakfasts. By signing up for Airbnb, you can earn money simply by renting out your unused space to travelers.

Obviously, there is some risk involved, but Airbnb has a community safety and standards expectations for people renting their space as well as those seeking places to stay. A form of government-issued identification is required so there isn't much to worry about in the way of hosting a felon. The site provides income examples, and a relatively easy search showed that one room in Denver, Colorado can go for as much as 250.00 per week. Not bad for passive income and the best part about this is, you already *own* the investment property.

Chapter 3 – Start a Blog

There are many things you can do with a blog, but we'll focus on two. Creating your own and buying an existing blog. Creating your own won't be entirely passive, but once again, it is easier than finding a part-time job. And with most passive income internet based ventures, you can do this from the comfort of your couch. You aren't going to miss out on cherished family time or dinner because you had to go from your full-time job to the part-time job.

The trick to blogging is consistency. Thousands of

blogs are created every year, and the majority of them are abandoned within a few months. Blogging is a competitive market and if it is something you choose to do, remember to stay consistent, post on a regular basis, market using other social media sites we've discussed previously. Passive income from blogging comes mostly from advertisements. Those big-time advertisers are looking for blogs that get a lot of traffic to advertise their product. This will require some work at the beginning with posting, marketing and reaching out to advertisers to get them to pay you to advertise on your blog. If you like to write, or you have an idea for something that's funny tech savvy, or just completely different, blogging is a great way to earn that semi-passive income.

To be clear, one can't expect to make decent passive income by writing and publishing any old blog. In my quest to find what people are most interested in reading about, I came across a list of a whopping *eighty-one* ideas for writing a blog that will sell. We won't be covering all, but I'm going to list the top ten.

1. **Self-improvement and Self-hypnosis**. Whether you go into a bookstore or are looking for books online, self-improvement is one that piques a lot of people's interest. No one is perfect, and most people are looking for a way to improve themselves. Whether it'd be through physical fitness or having a more positive attitude in life, there are literally hundreds, if not thousands of self-improvement topics to blog about. Self-hypnosis is incredibly interesting. It isn't what you think, either. We've all seen the silly reality shows where people using hypnosis make their subjects act out of sorts. Self-hypnosis in this context actually goes hand in hand with self-improvement. Self-hypnosis is about meditating your way to a different you. Whether you need to boost your self-esteem or work on confidence and overall outlook on life, self-hypnosis is something that people are highly interested in.

2. **Health and Fitness for Busy People**. This is kind of along the same lines as self-improvement.

Many people want to get in better shape, but who really has the time? A blog about fitness for people who are always on the go (and not working on earning passive incomes like we are) would be a great target audience. Plus, many sports and activity retailers would love to pay to advertise on a site that is suggesting people get into shape. Everything they need to attain their goals is a click away...from *your* blog.

3. **Language and Learning Blogs**. These can be lumped in with creating that online course we discussed earlier. As a matter of fact, should you choose to teach a course, you could include blogs from your personal site as part of the learner's course and content. The language might be a little more difficult if you are only fluent in one, but learning new things always appeals to people.

4. **Earning extra money**. Who better to write a blog about this subject than you? You're well on your way to earning passive income without having to

get a second job, right? There are quite a few blogs that discuss passive income, but there aren't many that detail trials, tribulations, and successes. It'd be a nice little niche for you to slide right into.

5. **Food blogs**. We aren't talking about the local pub or fast food chain. Specialty or unique/rare foods are what interests people. "Foodie" blogs come and go, but the same applies here as it did with fitness. Rating food and restaurants in a way that gets people to read your blog over others will entice advertisers to pay for space on your blog. And, you get to go out and try all kinds of amazing new foods. Sounds like a win-win situation.

So, we've talked about creating your own blog, but what if you aren't interested in writing them yourself? Perhaps you don't quite have the time to invest in doing some research and writing the blog, then finding advertisers for your site. That's okay; there is another way to earn a passive income by purchasing a pre-existing blog. The interesting thing about this idea is all the content is there. You will have to put some effort into maintaining the site, but all the bare bones are set up for you.

A lot of blogs use Google AdSense, which is what provides a monthly income for a blogger. It is based on the ads Google places on their site or blog. Blogs tend to sell for approximately twenty-four times their average monthly income. For instance, if a blog earns two-hundred and fifty dollars per month, the most you'll pay for that blog is three-thousand dollars. Like we mentioned in the chapter about investing in real estate, some things will require a bit of money up front. If you are able to afford this route with buying a blog, keep in mind that if the site is generating two-fifty per month, you will earn your money back in a year. After that, the blog will be making money that will be all profit. With a little effort put into the blog to make sure content remains up to date, it'll be mostly passive and something you can do in your spare time.

Chapter 4 – Selling Products Online

There are a couple of ways to make money by selling products online to earn a passive income. Actually, there are several, but the point of this book is passive income, so we will stick to discussing two great ways to make that money using a website. Drop ship products for another retailer, or sell your own products online. If you don't want to invest a lot of money in products to stock your online store, drop shipping might be more appealing. In this chapter, we will cover both so you can get a good idea as to what will work best for you and fit into your budget.

Drop shipping isn't entirely passive, but it's one of the closest things you can to do earn that passive income. What is it, you ask? Drop shipping is where a product goes directly from the manufacturer to the customer.

And, where do you fit into this equation? You would be the middle man. Drop shipping requires a little effort in that you'd need to set up a website to sell a product. What's particularly significant about this is, you don't have to spend the time creating a product, then marketing it online, calculating sales, paying people to help you out...none of that. The middle man in this scenario simply has the product on their site, and when people arrive to purchase, the order is either automatically or manually forwarded to the manufacturer. The product is then "drop shipped" to the customer. This means you will never have to get your hands dirty. The passive income part of this scenario comes from your earning a percentage of the sales of whatever product or products you have on your website.

In addition to simply being the middle man, let's talk about some other benefits to using drop shipping as your passive income source. One of the biggest advantages is that the startup for this is minuscule, especially compared to some of the other things we've mentioned such as real estate and purchasing a blog. You will also be able to offer an extensive selection and wide variety of products without ever having to purchase the product, store it, then pay to have it shipped to the customer.

The risk is reduced tremendously with drop shipping. Most retailers who set up a website and sell the product have to invest hundreds or even thousands of dollars up front to build their inventory. Drop shipping requires you purchase the product only briefly, then have it shipped directly to the customer. The upfront cost of drop shipping is pretty minimal. You also don't need to worry about renting space to house the product. The store you own is virtual which means you can run your drop ship business from the comfort of your own home. Or, anywhere that has wifi.

What's important to mention about drop shipping is if you want to be successful, you'll need to find a specialized niche. In order to do well with drop shipping, you'll want to do a little research and find retailers that utilize that service. Don't narrow yourself to one or two markets. In the beginning, start small, but the more you are able to expand and the more products you are able to add to your website, the more likely you are to earn a pretty decent passive income.

When it comes to selling your own products on the internet, the possibilities are endless. Online, you can sell any service or product that you can think of. It could be anything from a product you've created, things of a digital nature like software or DVDs, even instructional videos if you have them. If not, this is a great opportunity for you to create them, as discussed in the section regarding Udemy or YouTube videos.

If you don't have want to setup your own website, you can work with affiliates who are willing to sell your product for you. In this instance, it would be like your partner is the drop shipper or middle man and you are the retailer. Either way is perfectly acceptable and a great way to earn a passive income.

How much money you make depends on how much time you are willing to commit to this venture. One story that is particularly intriguing is that of a woman who was able to quit her job and earn one-hundred thousand dollars a year with her online store. Now, let's be clear that this isn't the norm. The reason she was able to make so much money was that she'd found that special niche. Her online store specializes in making handkerchiefs for special occasions like weddings. They don't just produce handkerchiefs, though. They make linen party favor bags, lace umbrellas, pillowcases and much more. That is the kind of idea that will earn significant money. Get those wheels in your head spinning! Undoubtedly you've had some magnificent ideas for products that are unique or even those that would simplify your daily life.

Along these lines, you can also set up a website to sell products that you are familiar with. This is similar to selling your own product except you don't have to create a product...you'll be selling someone else's product. With this concept, you could start out small with one or two products, and after a while, you can add other products that are closely related to what you've already begun to sell. You'd want to make the products similar to avoid needing a large website to sell hundreds of products.

Keeping your site neat, clean and straightforward will bring more traffic.

Chapter 5 – Affiliate Marketing

When it comes to passive income, the majority of people who get into it start out in affiliate marketing. While the concept has been around for quite some time, it became popular after the 4-Hour Work Week was released. Ever since then, people have been excited to find a way to "make money while they sleep." The idea behind affiliate marketing is you earn a commission by promoting other people's products. You make money when a sale is completed thanks to your marketing. This relies heavily on revenue sharing, which can go either way. That means that if you have a product and are looking to sell more of it, you can offer promoters financial incentive for marketing your product. Alternatively, if you do not have a product of your own, you can still make money by promoting a product you believe in or are familiar with.

In this chapter, we are going to get into detail as to what affiliate marketing is and how you can get started earning passive income by using it.

Conversely, there are three or four sides to affiliate marketing, depending on which definition you are looking at. For all intents and purposes, when it comes down to it, there are really only two sides to this marketing equation. There are the product seller and creator on the one hand and the marketer on the other. In affiliate marketing, you can be both the creator and the marketer and profit from 'shared' revenue.

Let's take a closer look at all the working parts of what makes affiliate marketing such a successful venture.

There is the merchant, who can also be the creator, seller, retailer, brand or vendor. Ultimately, the merchant is the creator of the product. For example, Dyson vacuum cleaners. On a smaller scale, it can be a person who creates and sells online courses to people wishing to further their education without having to go back to college. From the solo entrepreneur to online startup companies and even Fortune 500 companies, just about anyone can be the merchant who is behind the affiliate marketing system. The merchant doesn't have to be actively involved. They only have to be able to offer a product to sell.

The next party is the affiliate who is also sometimes referred to as the publisher. Like the merchant, the affiliate can be an entire company or an individual. The affiliate is where the marketing happens. They are the party responsible for promoting one or several products in an attempt to attract and even convince those potential customers that the product is needed or of great value and the customer winds up purchasing this product because of the marketing. One way this type of marketing is achieved is by a review of the product being sold with a blog. Really, this can be done on any social media outlet and Facebook is getting to be a huge platform for affiliate marketing. Perhaps you hadn't noticed it before, but you likely will now. Maybe one of your friends posted something about a product they liked. If you went to that website and bought a product, your friend might have been compensated and would be the affiliate.

Now, while there are two parties to the actual functionality of affiliate marketing, there is one key component to recognize, and that is the customer. Without people to consume the product, there would be no need for affiliate marketing, right?

The consumer or customer might be unaware that they are involved in affiliate marketing. That depends on how the affiliate markets the product. Some affiliates let their customers know up front that they are trying to sell a particular product. Others are more passive in using ads or links in their blogs for people to follow to certain websites. No matter how the consumer gets to the product, the affiliate is paid a commission if there is a sale, so long as there is an agreement between the affiliate and the merchant. Nine times out of ten, there is some sort of arrangement between the two parties. Most people don't tend to push a product without having an incentive to do so. Whether the affiliate gets paid in free product or cold hard cash is something to be worked out between the marketer and affiliate. If you choose to be an affiliate for a product to earn passive income, make sure your contract is clear so that no matter which form of payment is received, you will actually be compensated for your time and effort in marketing the product.

At the beginning of this chapter, we talked about three to four components to affiliate marketing. Because most people only see three true components, we will not go into too much detail with the fourth. However, it should be mentioned, albeit briefly.

The fourth component is the network. In most cases, the network acts as an intermediary between the merchant and the affiliate. The network tends to handle payment between the merchant and the affiliate. They can also be responsible for shipping and delivery of the product being sold. The use of a network is not required, although some bigger corporations tend to use the networks to promote, ship and deliver their product. A good example of a network is Amazon. That website sells everything you can think of from tools and books to toys and household items. They have an Amazon Associate program that allows you to promote any item you sell on their platform. Of course, Amazon charges a fee for this, though it is usually pretty minimal.

Now, there are four simple steps to becoming either a merchant or an affiliate. Most people begin with affiliate because it is slightly easier than starting out as a merchant. We will provide you with the four steps for each so that you can make an informed decision as to which route you'd prefer to take to start earning your passive income.

Becoming an Online Merchant in 4 steps:

1. You need to have an idea for a product. This is tough because many people have it in their head that coming up with an idea is hard, which isn't necessarily true. What happens with most people is they have an idea that they are in love with and that is where the problem is. They become too focused on that *one* idea. To get started as a merchant, you'll want to find products out there

that are already selling well, but that the market isn't already flooded with. You need something that people will want to buy and will be able to use on a daily basis. Perhaps you have an idea that will make household chores easier or a product that can clean as well as bleach without all the toxic fumes. Take a little bit of time and do some research on Google to find ideas or products you can get behind.

2. The second step is to validate your idea. You wouldn't want to make or back a product without knowing that there would be reasonable interest for people to purchase it. Ask family, friends, work associates...anyone you know will be *honest* with you about the product you are looking to sell. Sometimes, that can be tough with family and friends because they want to support you in your ventures. Make sure you are asking people you know will tell you the absolute truth.

3. Create your product or prepare to market the already established product you've decided to sell. Creating products can be costly up front. However, if you've done research, had plenty of people tell you they'd definitely buy it and you are passionate about it, go for it!

4. Finally, once your product is ready, you'll need to find the affiliates willing to sell and market your product on your behalf.

Becoming an Online Affiliate in 4 steps:

1. First and foremost, start reviewing the products in your chosen niche. You can do this via YouTube, a blog or live streams on a platform like Periscope.

2. Collect emails so that you can connect with your audience.

3. Check out joint venture webinars. It is a great platform to make a lot of sales in a shorter period of time. At the same time, you'll be growing your email list and expanding your customer base.

4. Finally, once you get your affiliate business to a point where it is making money you can scale growth by using pay per click advertising.

To recap, there are two ways to get into affiliate marketing; becoming an affiliate or becoming a merchant. With what we've outlined here today, I'm positive you'll be able to find which route works best for you. Perhaps you'll discover you can do both!

Chapter 6 – Venture Capitalism

Investopedia defines venture capitalism as a person who provides capital for startup ventures or one who supports small companies that want to expand but lack access to equities markets. Venture capitalists are people who are willing to invest in these companies because they know they will earn significant returns on the companies if they are successful. There is some risk in investing in companies that are in the startup phase because most new businesses fail within the first year. If it is a risk you are financially able to take, it's an easy way to earn a passive income. The venture capitalist provides the money up front, and when the business succeeds, they get to sit back and relax while the money rolls in.

While there are several paths to becoming a venture capitalist, there are two that are most common and, quite frankly, the simplest to get into. Serial entrepreneurship and tech-oriented investment banking.

The serial entrepreneur differs from a typical entrepreneur in that they will come up with an idea for business, get it started, and then hand the reigns over to someone else. An entrepreneur that is not serial will start a business, get it through the first year and beyond and stick with it until they retire or sell the business. Typically, they do not start more than one business whereas a serial entrepreneur will do this several times throughout their business life. This is ideal for people who have lots of great ideas and want to share them with the world. Once the business is up and running, the serial entrepreneur will earn a passive income from all the businesses they get started. Like many forms of passive income and as we've mentioned a time or two, getting on the road to passive income will take some work. Ultimately, when you are earning money without having to leave your home, whatever you put into the idea, in the beginning, will clearly be worth it.

In addition to the ability to spot a great investment from a mile away, a serial entrepreneur is also great at motivating people and inspiring others to follow them. They are willing to take a personal and business risk. They have the ability to recognize a great market to invest in consistently. Some people have made their career being a serial entrepreneur. Realistically, you could help several businesses get their start, which would not be passive. However, once those businesses are up, running and making good money, all you have to do is sit back and enjoy the fruits of your labor. And that, my friend, is the definition of passive income.

The second is the tech-oriented investment banker. Of the two, this is becoming less common because the risk associated is higher. An investment banker, in general, is someone who provides the capital for business...any business. Now, as we have mentioned previously, for this section, we are specifically talking about tech-oriented investments. These tend to be a little less risky because of the way technology is evolving. People are always looking for the next new, really impressive technological advancement. For this type of venture capitalism, you would invest in some kind of emerging technology, and when it succeeds, you will get to reap the rewards of getting in on this investment on the ground floor. As we have talked about previously, finding a specific niche or even an area of technology in which you are particularly well versed is a great way to keep your risk a little lower. That being said, you probably would not want to invest in several tech companies right away. The point of passive income is earned money with less stress than having to go out and find a part-time job. Do a little research on emerging technologies and find the one you are most confident in.

As we've gone over a few times so far, any kind of investing comes with risk. Of the two most common forms of investing through venture capitalism, you are more likely to succeed and experience less risk with serial entrepreneurship. That being said, if you are very tech savvy and can recognize a great product easily, go that route. Remember, you are trying to get yourself to a point where you are earning that passive income, and that means finding exactly what is going to work best for you.

Conclusion

Thank for making it through to the end of *Investor's Ultimate Guide From Novice to Expert: Invest Intelligently to Six Figures.* Let's hope it was informative and able to provide you with all of the tools you need to achieve your goals of doing well and making money with investing! If you found this information interesting or helpful, make sure to leave a review!

About The Author

Hi there it's Jonathan Walker here, I want to share a little bit about myself so that we can get to know each other on a deeper level. I grew up in California, USA, and have lived there for the better part of my life. Being exposed to many different people and opportunities when I was young, it made me want to strive to become an entrepreneur to escape the rat race path that most of my peers had taken. I knew I wanted to be able to travel and experience the world the way it was meant to be seen and I've done just that. I've travelled to most places around the world and I'm enjoying every minute of it for sure. In my free time I love to play tennis and believe it or not, compose songs. I wish you all the best again in your endeavours, and may your dreams, whatever they may be, come true abundantly in the near future.

CPSIA information can be obtained
at www.ICGtesting.com
Printed in the USA
LVHW080012121120
671417LV00015B/2088